I Enright

Library of Congress Cataloging-in-Publication Data
Enright, Elizabeth, 1909–1968.
Zeee/by Elizabeth Enright; illustrated by Susan Gaber.
p.   cm.—(An HBJ contemporary classic)
Summary: Zeee, a fairy whose homes are always being destroyed by
careless people, continually takes revenge on the hated humans until
she is befriended by a little girl who is the only person who can see her.
ISBN 0-15-299958-2
[1. Fairies—Fiction.] I. Gaber, Susan, ill. II. Title.
PZ7.E724Ze 1993
[Fic]—dc20   91-29611

First edition   A B C D E

HBJ

The illustrations in this book were done in watercolor
on Strathmore Bristol board.
The display type and text type were set in Perpetua
by HBJ Photocomposition Center, San Diego, California.
Color separations by Bright Arts, Ltd., Singapore
Printed and bound by Tien Wah Press, Singapore
Production supervision by Warren Wallerstein and Ginger Boyer
Design by Camilla Filancia and calligraphy by Judythe Sieck

ELIZABETH ENRIGHT

Illustrated by

SUSAN GABER

An HBJ Contemporary Classic

Harcourt Brace Jovanovich, Publishers

San Diego   New York   London

ZEEE was a bad fairy and proud of it. She lived alone and always had. She had no mother, father, sisters, brothers, uncles, aunts, or cousins and never had any. About a hundred years before this story begins, she had invented herself by magic. Before that she had been something else, but she couldn't remember what. Zeee did not look her age by any means. She looked exactly eight and a half years old—always had and always would—not one day more, not one day less. She was about the size of a bumblebee and could fly like one. She had stingers on the ends of her fingers; and on her forehead, two antennae, or feelers, that could tell her what day of the week it was, what time of day it was, and what sort of weather to expect. She also had a wise, quick mind of her own.

When I say that Zeee was bad, I mean she was bad about only one thing, and that was people.

She didn't care much for any of the extremely large live creatures that inhabited the part of the world she lived in. She held cows in contempt, thought horses dull, and scorned most dogs because they were always in an uproar about something or trotting about looking for something else and then forgetting what it was and lying down and going to sleep. Most of them lacked concentration. But though she did not care for these particular animals, she did not hate them.

She hated people.

She regarded people as unnecessarily large, cumbersome, and clumsy, and, rather like dogs, they were often in an uproar about something, and many of them lacked concentration. But what she hated most about people was the fact that they could never see her. They didn't even know that she was there. No matter how she screamed into their large curly ears or how she stung them with her sting-fingers, they never even noticed her enough to brush her away.

Everything else could see her: cows, toads, crickets, cats (of whom she was a little afraid), spiders, foxes, snails; everything but people. No wonder she hated them.

And then there was the matter of her houses and what became of them. She had been forced to move more often than she could possibly remember, and always because of some Person. Time and time again she had to take her little bits of furniture and leave a ruined dwelling place in search of a new one.

Her furniture was just the right size for her; and she was proud of it.

Every fall, for instance, she made herself a new bed. It was always a ripe milkweed pod neatly split down the center. It was shaped like a cradle and soft as a cloud inside: all the flosses were stitched in place so that they couldn't tickle or fly away. And every fall she gathered new blankets: leaves from the mullein plant, thick as felt, woolly and warm. Her table was a calico crab shell set on acorn legs. She had two fishbone footstools, a chair made out of birch twigs, and another made out of a walnut. She had a hammock of woven grass and three chrysalis lanterns. Her bathtub was a clamshell, her basin a thimble, her mirror a sequin. To decorate her walls (if the house happened to have walls), she used, among other things, the wing of a sulphur butterfly and an oriole's feather. She did not believe in curtains. When she had everything arranged, her houses were always pleasant and attractive. It was a pity that sooner or later every single one of them was ruined.

One particular summer, the summer of this story, Zeee had more than the usual series of household disasters. In June she had found the perfect little pagoda-tent of dock leaves just at the corner of the Blastovers' lawn. She moved her furniture in, settled down, and was very well satisfied. She enjoyed her tent in bad weather particularly, because the sound of the rain on a dock-leaf roof is one of the best sounds there is.

Mr. Blastover himself was a fat man, with a fat wife, a fat dog, and a fine fat lawn.

This lawn was the pride of his eye: it was green as an emerald and soft as the down on a duckling. Softer. Mr. Blastover was always mowing it and mulching it and watering it and weeding it. He even made his wife take her shoes off when she walked across it.

"High heels would ruin it," he said. "They would ruin a work of art!"

From her dock-leaf pagoda, Zeee watched them idly and laughed at them. She felt very superior to those big, fat people.

But one day Mr. Blastover, patrolling his precious lawn (in soft-soled bedroom slippers), noticed the dock leaves that reached out over a tiny corner of the grass.

"Now how did I miss those?" said he, and he whipped out his clippers and clipped them off, and there went Zeee's roof. It was only by luck that he didn't plant his large foot on her furniture and squash it flat.

Zeee in a perfect frenzy of rage flew straight at Mr. Blastover's ear and screamed into it, "Fat Mr. Blastover, I hate you! I loathe you! I detest and despise you!"

But of course he didn't hear a word. She stung his earlobe with her sting-fingers, but of course he didn't feel a thing, so she stung his dog instead. *He* felt it, all right, and ran away howling, which was some consolation but not enough. In the end, she went to her friend the mole, whose name was Sunderly, and told him what had happened.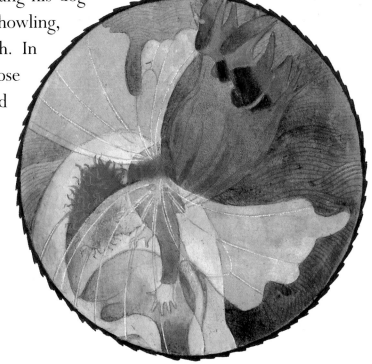

"A perfect lawn, you say?" said Sunderly, smiling his gentle smile and rubbing his little glovelike hands together. "A *perfect* lawn? Oh, what pleasure lies ahead! A thousand thanks, my dear."

And that night while Mr. Blastover lay fatly fast asleep, Sunderly and all his cronies descended upon the perfect lawn, descended *into* it, in fact, and started tunneling.

When Mr. Blastover woke up the next morning and strolled over to the window, the sight he beheld caused him to bellow with such force that all the dogs in the neighborhood began to bark, and Zee hugged herself with pleasure.

"Go and buy a dozen mole traps!" Mr. Blastover shouted from his window to the gardener. "Buy *two* dozen of them, and some poison!"

But by this time, Sunderly and all his friends had quietly departed and were safe.

Weary of lawns, Zeee decided to set up housekeeping near the sea. She was fortunate in finding a deserted sand pail that lay half-buried amongst the beach grass, well beyond reach of the tides. It was a perfect summer cottage: shady, cool, nicely painted with sailboats on the outside, and nicely painted plain blue on the inside. Every day she made a fresh carpet out of dusty-miller leaves, which are silver-gray in color and soft as Sunderly's velvet coat, very pleasing to a small bare foot. She enjoyed her cottage, especially in bad weather, because the sound of rain on a sand-pail roof is another of the best sounds there is.

The part of the shore that Zeee had selected was fairly deserted; people seldom came there, preferring to gather in clusters and bunches at the bathing beach two miles away.

But one day, in July, some people did come: a whole family of them, in fact, beginning with a father carrying a beach umbrella and a basket, continuing with a row of children, all sizes, carrying towels and bathing suits, and winding up with a mother carrying not one baby but two.

Zeee observed with horror that all the children were boys, and they turned out to be the sort who threw sand at each other, ducked each other, squabbled, tattled, and yelled.

"Boys! Boys!" the mother would call out now and then, but they paid no more attention to her than to the soft summer wind that was blowing.

"Now, fellows, cut that out!" the father would order from time to time, but after a second or two they paid no more attention to him than to the soft summer waves that were lapping the beach. Zeee huddled in the shade of her sand pail and glowered. She hated them all.

Suddenly, in a single dreadful second, one of the creatures broke away from his brothers and came galloping through the beach grass.

"Lookit what I found! A lost pail!" he shouted triumphantly, and before Zeee could escape, he had seized the handle of the pail and yanked it up, so that Zeee's floor of sand, her carpet of dusty miller, and all her furniture fell on top of her. Then the terrible boy

lifted the pail high above his head and whirled it around and around in a circle so fast that nothing fell out, including Zeee, until he stopped, and by that time she was so dizzy that her wings staggered and slammed her into a sand thistle.

Nursing her wounds furiously, Zeee watched the family unpack their picnic basket, and then, quicker than light, she went to her friend Nang, chief of the big black ants, and told him what had happened and what was happening.

"Peanut butter and bacon sandwiches?" said Nang, his large eyes glittering with anticipation. "Real hot dogs with real catsup? Real jelly doughnuts? Real chocolate-chip cookies? Ants of the region, fall in line. Charge!"

And the black ants filed in line by the hundreds, then by the thousands, and soon were swarming greedily all over the picnic lunch.

Just to be sure that true vengeance was hers, Zeee also mentioned the picnic people to her friend Zoan, the mosquito.

"Healthy little boys? Two smooth round babies? M-m-m," said Zoan. "Thank you, thank you. I'll tell my friends; mustn't be selfish. M-m-m," and she went wheening away with her thin legs dangling.

So the picnic family was defeated and in great haste, sorely bitten, packed up their things and ran away, rattling and complaining.

Zeee was also defeated, however, for the boy who had found her sand pail held on to it and took it home. The only other suitable place in the neighborhood to live in was a fisherman's boot, very old and dry. It smelled strongly of dead rubber and faintly of fish, and she had to share it with a spider, but at least it was a roof over her head; and the spider turned out to be good company.

But before very long, that household came to an end, too. The woman who owned the property went for a walk one day, discovered the boot, and holding it at a dainty distance, took it home and put it in the trash bin.

"It's the town dump for us next," said the spider cheerfully. "But what's the difference? Home's home, wherever they put it."

"Not for me," said Zeee. "I draw the line at living in a dump." And off she went house-hunting again, while the spider looked after her furniture.

Her next experience was one of her worst. Zoan had told her about a deserted wasps' nest hanging in a plum tree near a vacant house. It was shaped like a lopsided balloon, silvery gray, made of layers and layers of wasp paper. Of course, it had to be hollowed out, and that took many hours of work, but when it was finished, with a door and two windows, it was the most delightful house of all. It swung gently when the wind blew, and the papery walls rustled and shimmered, and it was a lovely place to sleep. Zeee was very happy there and flew in and out of her door or windows just as she chose, as much at home as the wasps had been.

A day came, however, when some people bought the old house, and peace was over. All at once there was a racket of hammers, a whine of saws, a shouting and gabble and loud singing from the workmen who were repairing the place. Also they brought their dogs with them, and the dogs barked. Zeee didn't mind any of that very much; she was rather fond of noise. But one day the young man and woman who had bought the house took a stroll about the gone-to-seed garden where the plum tree grew.

"Look, Patrick, roses!" cried the young woman in delighted surprise. "Yellow ones and pale pink, and all ours, waiting for us—and oh, look! A wasps' nest! It's like a big silver pear. . . . I've always wanted one of those. . . ."

"Have you, darling?" said the young man. "Wait here a moment."

Zeee stuck her tongue out at the young woman, closed her doors and windows, and sat down on the floor, scowling. What a fine world this would be if all the people would move off it, she thought. And then . . . but what was happening? Suddenly her house was full of smoke: chokingly, suffocatingly full. . . . Zeee gasped, coughed, sneezed, flung open her door, and, nearly dead, flew out.

There stood the abominable young man holding a torch of burning newspaper just below her house.

"You have to smoke them out," he was explaining to his wife.

"But I haven't seen a single wasp, have you?" she said. "Nothing has come out at all."

"Oh, yes it has, stupid," said Zeee. "*I've* come out." But of course the young woman never heard a word.

"I think it must be abandoned," said the young man, sounding rather disappointed. He tapped the wasps' nest gingerly. "Yes, it's empty."

"Thief, robber, murderer!" screamed Zeee at his healthy-looking ear. It didn't even twitch. "I *hate* you," she shouted.

The young man stamped out the torch and cut the wasps' nest, twig and all, from the plum tree.

"It will look lovely against the paneling in the dining room. Silver against gold," said the young woman, touching the paper nest with her finger.

"And *I hate you!*" shouted Zeee. "I hate you even worse!"

That night she had to fly into the people's house and remove her furniture piece by piece. It smelled horribly of smoke and would continue to do so for weeks. The only place she could find to put it was an empty pickle jar in a meadow. It was a slippery sort of place and not very private, not nearly so nice as the wasps' nest. Zeee was frustrated and furious, and this time she appealed to her friend, Slaith, the grass snake. He was perfectly harmless and very beautiful, Zeee thought, being without question the most exquisitely neat and graceful creature she knew. He was green as green water and slim as a ribbon, and nothing moved as wonderfully as he did, not even green water when it is moving. But Zeee knew how some people feel about snakes.

"Slaith, do you enjoy making people scream?" she asked him.

"I love it better than anything," Slaith said. "But unfortunately I'm harmless. How I wish I were a viper!"

"Come with me and you shall have a scream," Zeee promised, and she and Slaith, one flying, one gliding, went to the garden of the house with the plum tree, and they waited.

Zeee sat on a dried yarrow flower, springy and comfortable. Slaith curved himself into a small flat wheel and raised his head on its green stem of neck. His eyes were dark little diamonds, and his tongue, shaped like the stamen of a flower, flickered as he waited.

Soon the young woman came out of the house humming a tune. She was barefoot and walked lightly across the grass to the garden, where she stopped to smell a rose.

"Now!" commanded Zeee, angry and happy.

Slaith looked at the young woman's bare foot, smiled tenderly, then gliding in silent perfection, he approached the foot and slipped over the toes.

"*Help! Screech!*" screeched the young woman, bounding into the air. Then she ran toward the house.

"Noisy things, aren't they?" Slaith said contemptuously.

"Noisy and stupid," Zeee agreed. "But now we must hurry away because she will call her husband, and he'll try to kill you. He seems to like killing things."

So she and Slaith, one flying, one gliding, returned to the meadow and the pickle jar.

"It was lovely how you made the Person yell," Zeee said admiringly. "It was gorgeous."

"I enjoyed it; oh, how I enjoyed it!" replied Slaith with his icy little smile. "It made me *feel* like a viper!"

The worst day, the very worst day, was the one when the tractor came into the meadow.

Zeee, who had been sitting in her doorway making a dress, heard it first: a grinding, stuttering noise that rocked the pickle jar. Then she saw it, towering against the sky, red as a dragon, and smelling of iron.

She had just time enough to spring into the air and out of the way when the tractor's mighty treads ground over the pickle jar, shattering it to bits, and with it all Zeee's furniture and clothes: all her little cups and dishes and her sand-grain jewelry.

And this time she was too discouraged even to be angry. She was too discouraged

even to cry (and, as a matter of fact, she could not cry because she had never learned how).

Nor did she go this time to Sunderly or Nang or Zoan or Slaith. She did not want revenge but only to be left in peace. She sat in a dried-up nest of gone-to-seed Queen Anne's lace and thought of all her ruined houses, not only those of this summer but also the other ones: the seashell that had been collected and put in a museum; the watering can that had suddenly and dreadfully been filled with water; the oriole's nest that had been gathered by a boy; and all the others, every one of which had been robbed or ruined by a Person.

So it was strange that when, later on, a sudden rain came pouring down, she did what she had never done before: she took refuge in a house belonging to a Person.

Well, it wasn't really a house but a sort of barn with wheelbarrows and garden tools inside it. Zeee was so worn out with discouragement that she could scarcely fly. Sadness always weakened her wings, though anger never did. Forlorn and dejected, she crawled into a tipped-over flowerpot, curled up, and went to sleep. The rain droned on the roof, droned and slowed and finally stopped. The sun came out, and a bold rainbow stood in the sky, though no one saw it.

A cat came out of the house near the barn and walked with distaste across the soaking grass. Every now and then he would stop with a disgusted look and shake the wetness from a paw. He was on his way to the barn, where occasionally he had found a mouse and where he hoped to find one today, for he was sick to death of cat food.

He walked his smoothly sloping walk to the barn, paused, sniffed, twitched. . . . What was *that?* Something with wings but not a bird, something alive but not a mouse. The cat sloped quietly over to the flowerpot, reached in a paw. . . .

Zeee opened her eyes and screamed. The velvet paw drew back, and in that instant of release Zeee sprang from the flowerpot, flying weakly and not high enough, flying by accident into a spiderweb, where she was caught fast.

"Look out!" said the spider who owned the web. "You're not edible and you're too heavy. You'll ruin the structure!"

He was a large spider, hairy and cross, not at all like the cheerful occupant of the boot, but Zeee pleaded with him.

"Help me out of this," she begged. "Please, please, help me out!"

"Why, what's up?" inquired the spider; then he saw the cat, and being cowardly as well as ugly, he scrambled up his tough silk ladder to a rafter, where he squatted, watching.

The cat—huge to Zeee—came crouching forward, very low, almost on his stomach; one paw lifted then set down without a sound. One velvet paw and then another, and his tilted eyes, yellow as fire, stared at her—nearer and nearer.

"Do you taste like mouse?" the cat asked softly.

"No! Like peppers and nettles and cinders and salt. I'll burn your tongue," Zeee said, although she hadn't the slightest idea how she tasted.

"I don't believe you," said the cat. "Perhaps you taste like bird."

He was nearly upon her now. He knew she couldn't get away, and his brilliant eyes looked interested and glad. Zeee struggled no longer; she could not move. If she had been able to remember any magic, she might have been able to turn herself into something else, but fear had frozen all the magic in her mind. The cat raised a triumphant paw.

"No! Stop!" cried a voice suddenly, and down from above came a hand, a Person's hand. It clutched the cat by the back of the neck and lifted him up, gently but firmly. "You are never to harm her as long as you live; now go away."

"Oh, cuttlebones," muttered the cat disgustedly, and he tramped out of the barn, tramped almost heavily, in a way he had when he was angry.

The Person was a child. She sat down on her heels, close to Zeee. Her long hair fell forward like tassels on her shoulders. Her eyelashes were thick and long, and between the lashes her gray eyes, clear as rainwater, looked down, looked at *her*. Zeee, who had never been looked at by a Person before, found that it was entirely different from being looked at by a cat, a snake, a fox, or any other living being.

"Who are you?" said the Person, and she said it quietly because she was astonished, and she smiled with joy because what she had always suspected was true, though everyone had told her that it wasn't. There *was* magic in the world after all.

"Can you see me? What do I look like?" asked Zeee, still half unable to believe. "Can you hear me?"

"I can see you and I can hear you," said the Person. "You're about the size of a bumblebee, and you have wings—lucky—but you're caught in a cobweb. Let me set you free."

Very gently the Person tore away the sticky web, strand by strand, while the spider glowered from his rafter, and at last Zeee was released. She smoothed out her dress, removed a filament of web from her antennae, and looked up at the Person with curiosity.

"Who are *you?*" she asked in turn, and the Person answered, "My name is Pandora. Pandora Smith. What's yours?"

"I think it's Zeee," said Zeee.

"It doesn't sound like a name," Pandora said. "It sounds more like a bee or my father's electric razor. My best friend that moved away was named Hope. Shall I call you Hope?"

Zeee thought about it.

"All right," she said. "You can if you want to. Nobody else will."

"I'm eight and a half. How old are you?"

"I'm eight and a half, too," Zeee said. "I've been eight and a half for years."

"Where do you live?" was Pandora's next question; and then Zeee told her about her many household tragedies, one after another.

"And all because of people," she said at the end, almost accusingly. "People! Because they couldn't see me. I don't know why *you* can."

"I don't either," said Pandora. "But I'm glad. And you know something? I have a house for you to live in. It's my doll's house, and it has everything: wall-to-wall carpeting and a television set—toy. Of course, the furniture will be a little big."

"But what about that cat?" said Zeee.

"Oh, *he* won't bother you again. He knows better now."

"And what about when you grow up?" inquired Zeee. "That's another thing about people. They're always growing up."

"We'll be friends even then," Pandora promised. "And my children will be your friends, and you can live in the doll's house forever."

Zeee relaxed and became a little less thorny.

"Well, thank you," she said. "And thank you for saving my life. Of course, there are certain things that I can do for you, too. I can tell you what dogs talk about, and moles and birds and rabbits. I can translate the language of caterpillars (they always talk with their mouths full), and I'm very good at finding things because I'm so close to the ground: things that people like, like pennies. And I can predict the weather and tell time without a clock."

"You're magic, Hope," Pandora said. "And you're my friend."

Zeee did not tell her right away, since she was still a little shy and thorny, that she felt very happy, that she hadn't known she had been lonely until she wasn't lonely anymore. Suddenly her wings were strong again. She flew briskly into the air, lighted on Pandora's shoulder, and they both laughed.

So from then on Zeee had a splendid house to live in, and she proved to be a proud housekeeper. She had everything she wanted, and even the cat respected her and left her in peace.

But sometimes, because she was a wild, free creature, Zeee would take a vacation from her respectable mansion and go camping for a while in an old tin can or a pop bottle or a scarecrow's pocket. In the end, however, she always returned to Pandora, who was her dearest friend.

And because at last she had a Person for a friend, she never hated people anymore.